Romans, Saxons & Vikings

Living in

R_oman Britain

Martyn Whittock

First published in Great Britain by
Heinemann Library
Halley Court, Jordan Hill, Oxford OX2 8EJ
a division of Reed Educational & Professional
Publishing Ltd.

MELBOURNE AUCKLAND
FLORENCE PRAGUE MADRID ATHENS
SINGAPORE TOKYO CHICAGO SAO PAULO
PORTSMOUTH NH MEXICO
IBADAN GABORONE JOHANNESBURG
KAMPALA NAIROBI

Designed by Ken Vail Graphic Design

Illustrations by Ken Vail Graphic Design

Produced by Magnet Harlequin

Printed in Hong Kong

03 02 01

10 9 8 7 6 5 4 3

ISBN 0 431 05963 2

This title is also available in a hardback library
edition (ISBN 0 431 05964 0).

British Library Cataloguing in Publication Data

Whittock, Martyn J. (Martyn John)
Living in Roman Britain. – (Romans, Saxons,
Vikings)
1. Great Britain – History – Roman period, 55 B.C.
– 449 A.D. – Juvenile literature 2. Great Britain –
Social life and customs – To 1066 – Juvenile
literature
I. Title II. Series 936.1'04

942.01

Acknowledgements

The Publishers would like to thank
the following for permission to
reproduce photographs.

Bignor Roman Villa: p.12; British
Museum: p.5, p.6, p.7, p.20, p.24,
p.26; English Heritage: p.8, p.11, p.16,
p.18; Janet & Colin Bord/Fortean
Picture Library: p.5; Reading Borough
Council: p.14; University of Newcastle
upon Tyne Audio Visual Centre: p.28

Cover photograph reproduced with
permission of The British Museum.

Our thanks to Dr Stephen Ridd and
Andrew Houghton for their comments
in the preparation of this book.

We would like to thank the following
schools for valuable comments made
regarding the content and layout of
this series: Fitzmaurice Primary
School, Bradford-on-Avon, Wiltshire;
Tyersal School, Bradford, Yorkshire.

Details of written sources

A. Rivet, C. Smith, *Place Names of
Roman Britain*, Batsford 1979: 1D; 9B

P. Salway, *Roman Britain*, Oxford
University Press 1981: 1A

**For Rebecca Whittock, with love
from Uncle Martyn.**

Contents

Clues from the past

Britain became part of the Roman Empire in AD43. It stayed part of the Empire until AD410. Many kinds of clues survive from this time, but we have to be careful how we use them.

Many clues survive from the times of the Romans. There are many clues available because:

- There were **industries** in Britain during Roman times, making more things than ever before.

- Britain became part of a large **Empire**. Things were brought to Britain from all over this Empire.

- The Romans brought new ideas about making buildings out of stone. These last longer than buildings made from wood.

Written words from the past

Before the Romans came to Britain, people here did not read or write. This changed when Britain became part of the Roman Empire. For the first time, people in Britain wrote about what life was like – but can we always trust them? Very few people could write, so we only know the ideas of a few people. It is only through writing that we can find out what people thought. We have more evidence about what people made, than about what they thought and felt.

Source A

In order to encourage rough men who lived in scattered settlements to live in peace, enjoying the pleasures of life, Agricola urged them to build [stone] temples, and houses.

*The Roman writer Tacitus tells how a Roman **Governor**, Agricola, tried to make British people live like Romans. It was written in about AD100. Tacitus married the daughter of Agricola. He might have been trying to please Agricola by writing this.*

Source B

Part of the north gate of a Roman fort at Housesteads, in Northumberland. Buildings made from stone last a long time, but a lot of the walls have been broken down. It is not easy to know what the whole fort looked like.

Source C

A silver jug. It comes from Water Newton, in Cambridgeshire. The Romans made many fine things, but ordinary people would not have had jugs like this.

Source D

Britain lacks sunshine. It is restored by the warmth of the sea flowing round it.

A description of Britain written by the Roman Minucius Felix, in about AD200. We do not know if he ever came to Britain himself.

Roman place-names

During the time that Britain was in the Roman Empire, the Romans gave names to many places. They were in the Latin language.

Some of the names of places in Roman Britain were new names. They were made up after the Romans made Britain part of the Roman **Empire**. Some of the names were old names. These places had been called by their names before the Romans took over Britain. These old names were then written down in Latin. This was the Roman language. British people began to speak this, too. Many soon spoke and lived like Romans.

Roman place-names today

Very few modern place-names date from Roman times. Most Roman place-names were changed after Britain stopped being part of the Empire. New people, called the **Anglo-Saxons**, came to Britain. They replaced Roman names with their own names. Most of our modern place-names are Anglo-Saxon names, but some Roman names can still be found today. Some still look a lot like their Roman names. Some have changed over the years.

Source A

The Rudge Cup. This was a souvenir from Hadrian's Wall, in Northumberland. It has the names of five forts on it. We know these are names of forts from things written by other Romans.

Source B

This is a letter written in about AD100. It is written in ink, on a very thin piece of wood. It is very hard to read. A special light has to be used so that the old ink will show up. The last line says: 'I am writing this to you from Vindolanda'.

How do we know?

Source A shows that some Roman place-names were recorded on souvenirs. These were made for people visiting Britain. We can use this evidence to find out the names of the forts and **settlements** along Hadrian's Wall.

Source B is from a letter which mentions the place where the person was living. This letter tells us the name of the fort, Vindolanda. This place was a fort on Hadrian's Wall.

Some modern place-names from Roman times

- Aust in Avon from the Latin name 'Augusta'
- Catterick in Yorkshire from 'Cataractonia'
- Lincoln from 'Lindum Colonia'
- London from 'Londinium'
- Portsmouth may be from the Latin name 'Portus'

Where Roman names were written

We know about Roman names because they were written down in various places. Some were written on stones on new Roman buildings. Some were written in letters. Some were written on souvenirs from Roman Britain. Some were written in Roman books about Roman history and geography.

Roman life in the countryside – villas

Most people in Roman Britain lived in the countryside. Many rich landowners lived in large houses in the country. These were called villas.

Before the Romans came to Britain, there were rich people who lived in the countryside. Some of the richest of them lived in round wooden houses in defended **settlements**. These were sometimes built inside **hillforts**.

Source A

*The remains of a Roman villa. This one is at Lullingstone, in Kent. It had many rooms, **mosaic** pavements and stairs down to a private room underground. This room was used for religious worship. The mosaics were made of tiny pieces of stone and tiles. They were put together to make patterns and pictures.*

Copying Roman ideas

When Britain became part of the Roman **Empire,** these rich British people wanted to live like Romans. They copied the ideas and fashions of their new rulers. One of the things they copied was living in **villas**.

What was a Roman villa?

Villas were large houses in the countryside. They were built from stone, with many rooms. They were often richly decorated. They often had mosaics on the floor, and painted walls. They often had underfloor central heating and bath houses. Most villas were surrounded by farmland run from the villa.

Source B

I would rather go abroad with my friend, than enjoy broad acres, animals for ploughing and a villa on the outskirts of town.

This is from a poem by a Roman called Horace. It tells us that Romans thought villas were country houses. It was written in the first century BC.

How do we know?

Source B shows what a Roman writer thought a villa was. He thought it should be in the countryside, with farmland around it. But it might be quite close to a town.

Source A shows that some villas were very large indeed. From it we know they were built out of brick and stone. They had many rooms. Some rooms were even below the ground. This villa has mosaics on the floors in some rooms.

Roman life in the countryside – poorer people

Ordinary people did not live in villas. They lived in farms and small villages. These were not built in Roman styles.

Most Roman **villas** were built in the south and east of Britain. Away from this area, people's lives were less changed by Roman ideas. Even in this area, poorer people copied fewer Roman ideas.

The farmhouses of poorer people

Poorer people often continued to live in houses like the ones used before the Romans arrived. These houses were often round. They were made from wood and thatch. They did not have **mosaics**, or many rooms. These people probably worked on the large villa **estates**.

Some changes in the countryside

Better-off farmers may have lived in rectangular wooden houses. These people copied some Roman ideas about houses, but they were not wealthy enough to make their homes as comfortable as the rich villas. They may have rented land from the villa owners.

Places where Roman villas were built

This map shows where most villas were in Roman Britain. There were large parts where there were no villas. Here people lived in houses that were not so rich. These houses did not change so much when the Romans began to rule Britain. Even where there were many villas, most people lived in much poorer houses.

A village lived in by poorer farmers. This is at Chysauster, in Cornwall. There were eight houses here. Each house was round. They were like houses built before Britain became part of the Roman **Empire**. People lived here in the first and second centuries AD.

How do we know?

Source A shows us that the houses of some people were not changed by the Romans taking control of Britain. These houses were round, not square. They did not have mosaics. They did not have richly decorated rooms.

The map was made from archaeological evidence around Britain. It shows that villas were not found in all parts of the country. The Romans did not change the whole of the countryside.

The growth of Roman towns

Romans built the first real towns in Britain. They ruled the country from these towns. They were also places to trade in.

Today we take towns for granted. They are places where many people live together. They have large churches, shops and offices. They have places to buy and sell things. But before the Romans, there were no British towns like this.

Roman ideas about towns

Before the Romans took control of Britain, there were places where many people came together to live and **trade**. Some were in places called **hillforts**.

Source A

*Part of the Roman wall at the town of 'Eburacum' (York). The bottom half of the wall is Roman. The top half was added when York was again a **fortified** city after the end of Roman Britain.*

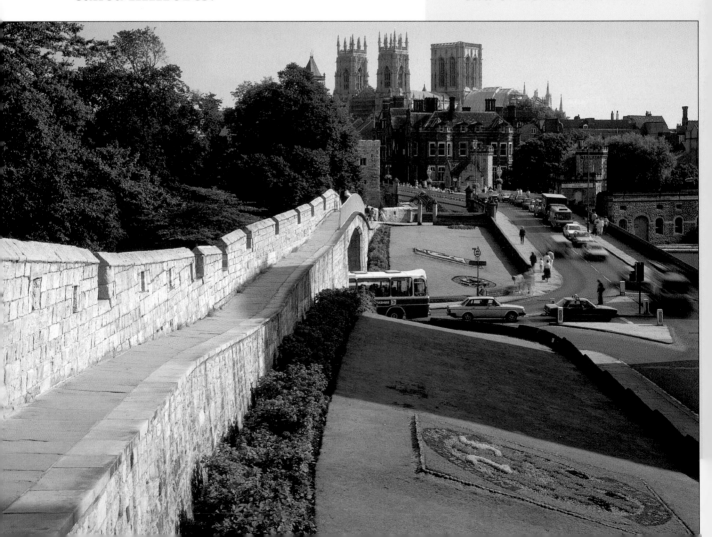

To the Romans, a town needed buildings made of stone. It needed temples, in which to worship Roman gods, baths and theatres, and large, impressive government buildings. The Romans wanted to encourage the building of towns in Britain. They thought this would make the British live like Romans. Then they would be happy, being members of the **Empire**.

The first Roman towns

The first Roman town was set up at Colchester, in AD49. It was called 'Camulodunum' by the Romans. The people living there were retired soldiers from the Twentieth **Legion**.

Britain had many different tribes and rulers when it became part of the Empire. The Romans encouraged the tribes' rulers to build towns from which the local area could be run.

Defended towns

The first Roman towns were not usually defended. Britain was peaceful. But from about AD100, people in towns began to build walls as defences. This spread after AD200. The new walls kept towns safe when there was trouble. They also made people in towns feel more important. Even after the Romans left Britain, these defences still attracted people to live in the old Roman towns.

How do we know?

Source A shows that Roman towns were defended by stone walls. It also shows how well these walls were made. They are over 1,500 years old and still standing.

This also shows that later people were attracted to live in towns like this because they had Roman walls. Later people used the old Roman walls. They rebuilt them and lived behind them.

13

Living in Roman towns

Roman towns offered people the chance to live more interesting lives. They had a chance to experience things they would never have seen in the countryside. They also offered them a chance to make money.

People had to come into towns to pay their **taxes** to the Roman government. They would sell the things they had grown, or made, for coins. They then paid their taxes. All of this made towns good places to buy and sell things.

Source A

Part of the walls of public buildings still standing at Wroxeter, in Shropshire. This was the Roman town of 'Viroconium'. The walls are still standing, over 1,500 years after they were built.

Planned streets and shops

Roman streets were carefully laid out. Gravel was used to make the roads. On either side of the roads there were drains. There were blocks of land between the streets. These were where the shops and houses were built.

The shops often had narrow fronts facing onto the street. More important ones had store-rooms, workshops and living rooms behind.

The forum and basilica

At the centre of the town was the market place, or 'forum'. Close-by was the 'basilica'. This was the public hall where the people met who ran the local area. These were the **magistrates** and the local council. There were also large temples, where Roman gods were worshipped. Theatres provided entertainment for the townspeople.

The public buildings of the town were made from brick and stone. They were large and very impressive. They were built to last a long time.

Toilets and sewers

The largest towns had toilets with flowing water. The water often had to be brought a long way to the town. There were sewers to take dirt and rubbish away. The sewers at 'Eburacum' (York) were large enough to walk through! Also, there would be public baths.

How do we know?

Source A shows that the Romans built public buildings out of brick and stone. It took a lot of skill and many people to build them. We know they were public buildings because they were part of a huge **bathhouse**. These were open to the public.

They were very large and meant to impress people. They were so well built that parts of them have lasted well over 1,500 years.

But it can still be hard trying to imagine what these buildings looked like. A lot of the building is no longer there.

Public entertainment

The Romans believed that people needed entertainment. There were many kinds of public entertainment in town.

Bath houses

A popular way to relax was a visit to the baths. This was an idea brought to Britain by the Romans. Most baths were public. Some smaller ones may have been private baths. The army had baths for its soldiers. One has been found at Caerleon, in Wales.

Source A

*A **mosaic** from the floor of a Roman **villa**. The villa is at Bignor, in Sussex. The mosaic shows two gladiators fighting. One is a 'secutor'. He has a short sword and a shield. The other is called a 'retiarius'. He is armed with a trident.*

How do we know?

Source A shows us the kinds of weapons used by Roman gladiators. Some used short swords, others had tridents. It also shows that the Romans liked to see different kinds of gladiators fight.

There is a ring in a stone between the gladiators. Gladiators who did not want to fight were tied to this ring. Then they had to fight.

This picture was put on a villa floor. This shows how popular watching gladiators was.

Source B shows that some gladiators fought to entertain Roman soldiers.

The baths were like modern leisure centres. They had sports grounds. Here people could play ball-games, run, box or wrestle. There was often an open-air swimming pool, and there were hot, warm and cold indoor baths, too. Food and drink could be bought at the baths.

Theatres

Theatres were used for religious celebrations and plays, which attracted many people. The seats were in a semi-circle, facing the stage.

Gladiators

The Romans liked to watch people fight. These people were **slaves**, called 'gladiators'. They usually fought to the death. Often, fighting gladiators had different kinds of armour. Some fought with short swords and shields. Others fought with three-pronged weapons, called 'tridents'. The fighting often took place in a round area called an 'amphitheatre'. There were seats on the bank around the fighting area.

Strangely enough, only one piece of gladiator armour has been found in Britain. This is a helmet. It was found at Hawkedon, in Suffolk.

Private entertainment

Not all Roman entertainment was public. A lot was private. This only involved people's families and friends. Rich people had most opportunity for relaxing.

Dinner parties

Rich people liked to give meals for their friends, in the afternoon. Ordinary people would be working then. Most of the decorated rooms in **villas** were probably used for these meals. There were usually three courses of food. For poorer people there were cafés and wine shops in the towns. These were like modern cafés and pubs.

Source A

Pieces of a board game. The board is made from a tile. The playing pieces are made from pottery, tile and glass. They come from Silchester, in Hampshire. This was the Roman town of 'Calleva'.

How do we know?

Source A shows us that board games were played by the Romans. The board was sometimes made from a tile. Lines were scratched on it to help make the game. This one had the lines put on it before it was **fired**. It may have been made to sell.

This source also shows that different materials were used to make the counters. These counters were made from pottery, tile and glass. But we do not know the rules of this game, or what it was called.

Source B shows how popular wine drinking was.

Board games

Many board games have been found from Roman Britain. These were probably enjoyed by rich and poor people. Boards were often made by scratching lines on tiles. The playing pieces were made from pieces of **pottery**, bone, lead or glass. Some pieces found at Silchester had words scratched on them. One had 'thief'. One had 'warlike'. One had 'first'. But we do not know what game they were from.

Music

A number of musical instruments have been found at Roman sites. Some were flutes made from bone. At Ashton, in Northamptonshire, a wooden reed pipe was found down a well. Rattles have also been found. These were called 'sistra' by the Romans. They were often used in Roman religious services.

Hunting

This was also very popular. Deer, hares and wild boar were hunted. Bears may have been hunted, too. Like board-games and music, hunting was probably enjoyed by rich and poor people, but probably only rich people could afford the dogs needed to catch the biggest animals.

Mining and quarrying

The Romans used a lot of stone for roads and buildings. They dug lots of it out of the ground. They also dug up gold, silver, copper, lead, iron, tin and jet.

The Romans were not the first people to do this. British people had done it for many years, but they were not as well organized as the Romans. The Romans knew there were useful stones and metals in Britain. This was one of their reasons for invading Britain.

Roman lead mines

Before the Romans landed in Britain, British people had mined lead on the Mendips, in Somerset. Soon after the Romans invaded Britain, their army captured these lead mines for the Roman government. All this lead had an official stamp put on it. British people probably also mined tin in Cornwall.

Britain has gold and silver and other metals, which belong to whoever is victorious.

Cornelius Tacitus, a Roman historian. He lived from about AD56–115.

How do we know?

Source B shows that the Romans thought that Britain had useful metals. They thought that whoever captured Britain could use them. This tells us that having these metals was one reason Romans invaded Britain.

Source A shows that the Roman government took over the Mendip lead mines. It also shows the name of the Roman man who ran the mines for the government, and it shows that silver was also found at these mines. This tells us that Romans mined lead and silver in Somerset.

Quarrying stone

Digging stone from the ground is called 'quarrying'. The stone was cut into the right shapes by hand. Metal wires were used to cut the stone. Wet sand helped the wire cut the stone.

Roman soldiers also dug stone from beside the roads that they were making. This stone was crushed and used as gravel on top of the road.

Special kinds of stone were quarried, too. Black Kimmeridge **shale** and Whitby **jet** were used to make furniture and jewellery.

Precious metals

Romans mined gold at Dolaucothi, in North Wales. Lead was heated to get silver from it. The work was done by **slaves** and prisoners. These were people who had been captured in wars, or punished for breaking the law.

Other metals

Lead was probably dug in the Pennines, as well as on the Mendips. Copper was dug in Shropshire and in Wales. Tin was found in Cornwall. Iron **ore** was heated to make iron that could be used by blacksmiths.

Workshops and craftworkers – pottery

People had made pottery in Britain for thousands of years before the arrival of the Romans. But the Romans organized it better than it had ever been before.

The Roman army needed **pottery.** As trade grew, ordinary people wanted more pottery, too. All kinds and styles of pottery were made, and it was cheaper than before.

Pottery was very important. Things made from pottery were used as cups, bowls and plates. It was used for cooking food. It was used as ornaments. It was even used for holding the ashes of dead people. Pottery had many different uses.

Source A

Different types of pottery from the Roman town of 'Verulamium' (St Albans), in Hertfordshire. Some of it was made in this country. Some was brought here from what is now modern France and Germany. Some pots were simple. Some were decorated. The pots were made in different colours and shapes.

One pot is decorated with the words 'DA MERVM' – 'Give me strong wine'.

How do we know?

Source A shows us that Roman potters made many different kinds of pots. Pots were made in different shapes. This probably depended on what they were used for.

These pots were made in different colours. Some are plain. Others are decorated. The words on one pot show that it was used for holding wine. It also shows that some pots were brought here from other countries.

Source B shows that potters wanted people at markets to know who made their pots.

Making pots

Pottery is made from clay. Roman potters sometimes added crushed grit, shells and sand to the clay. This stopped the pot from cracking when it was **fired**.

This clay was shaped and put in a kiln. This was like an oven. The clay pot was fired. This means that the clay was heated up. This made it go very hard.

The changing pottery industry

At first, most of the work was done by small groups of potters. They made pots for their local area. Over time, many of these groups joined together. These groups were better organized. They made thousands of pots. They sent them greater distances to sell them in markets. By AD300, four main pottery firms were making most pots used in Britain.

Different types of pottery

There were different shapes and types of pot. Some were cheap. Most people could afford these. They were sometimes dark in colour. They had no decoration. Other pottery cost more. It was sometimes red. Some pots had patterns or pictures on them.

Workshops and craftworkers – expensive jewellery and ornaments

Some Roman craftworkers made beautiful jewellery and ornaments. This took a lot of time. It needed expensive metal and jewels. Objects like these could only be bought by rich people.

Rich people in Roman Britain wanted to show how wealthy they were. This was not new. Rich people had done this before the Romans came to Britain. But the new Roman skills and **trade** allowed rich people to buy more impressive things than before.

Some **pottery** was so expensive that only rich people could afford it. But the most expensive objects were things made from silver and gold.

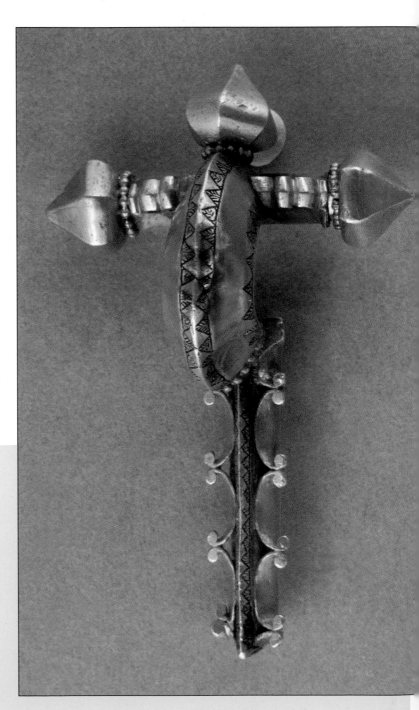

Source A

*A crossbow **brooch**. It is made from gold. It was found in Scotland.*

A gold necklace. It is made with precious stones, called carnelians, and with blue paste (used to make artificial jewels) and gold wire. It was found in Wales.

Expensive jewellery

Brooches were often made by pouring gold into moulds. This is called 'casting'. Bracelets and necklaces often used precious stones, or a type of glass which looked like a precious stone. This is called 'paste'. They were often decorated with gold wire.

Other rich ornaments

Rich people could also buy vases and jugs made from glass. Glass was hard to make, and it cost a lot. The best glass came to Britain from what is now Germany, and the Middle East.

Rich people could also buy plates and dishes made from silver. These were sometimes decorated with pictures of Roman gods, or other scenes.

How do we know?

The jewellery in Sources A and B show that **craftworkers** in Roman Britain were skilled at making beautiful objects. It shows that some of these were made with gold, and with precious stones. The gold was sometimes 'cast' in a mould, or used as a fine wire. This shows the kinds of skills used in making jewellery. A special kind of glass was used in the necklace. It is called 'paste'.

Women in Roman Britain

Women in Roman Britain were often under the control of men. Women ran their homes. Life was hardest for poor women.

Marriage and home life

Most women would have been married by the time they were 16 years old. Their husbands were chosen by their parents.

Women were under the control of their husbands, but they had power over their homes. This included cooking and looking after children. Richer women had slaves to do the work for them.

Poor women

Poorer men and women would have been the **slaves** for richer people. The hardest jobs were done by slaves. Many would have been women. They belonged to their masters and mistresses.

Source A

A statue of a priestess. Her head is covered, probably because she took part in religious ceremonies. The statue comes from South Shields, in Northumberland.

Many ordinary women would have worked with the rest of their family on the farm, in the shop, or making things to sell.

Rich women

Rich women had time to take care of their appearance. They owned perfume flasks. They owned mirrors and combs. **Archaeologists** in York found a woman's body where the hair was still on the skull. It was carefully braided. It was kept in place with pins made from **jet**. The hair had been dyed red. Only rich women could afford to dress like this.

Women and religion

Some women became priestesses in one of the different religions in Roman Britain. They probably helped **sacrifice** animals to the gods, and they probably helped in the other ceremonies in the temple.

Other women might pay for an **altar** to be set up to one of the many gods. One of these altars has been found at Greta Bridge, in Yorkshire. It was paid for by a woman named Brica and her daughter Januaria.

Part of the Empire

Britain was part of the Roman Empire. The Empire covered a huge area, from Britain to the Middle East. This meant that people could buy and sell things in Britain which had come from all over the Empire.

The **Empire** made **trade** easier. The Roman army made the Empire peaceful. It was easier to travel on the new Roman roads. Towns were good places for trade.

Foreign goods in Britain

Many things were brought to Britain from across the Empire. The most expensive glass bowls and jars came from the Middle East. Some came from what is now Germany. Some German glass was brought by merchants who traded with the north of Britain.

Source A

A glass bowl and a jug found at Radnage, in Buckinghamshire. They were made at Alexandria. This is in Egypt, in the Middle East.

How do we know?

Sources A and B show us that goods were brought to Britain from across the Roman Empire. The two glass objects came all the way from Egypt.

The British person who bought them would have paid a lot of money for them. This made it worth bringing them all the way from Egypt.

Because they were glass, they would have been easily broken. Great care must have been taken in bringing them to Britain.

Pottery called 'Samian ware' was brought to Britain from what is now France. A cargo of this pottery was lost when a ship sank at the mouth of the River Thames. It has been found by modern **archaeologists**. It was worth bringing things so far because a lot of money was paid for them. This made it worth all the effort.

Olive oil, wine and fish sauce came from hotter countries. A large wine jar found at the Roman town of 'Corinium' (Cirencester) shows it came from Spain.

British goods across the Empire

Jet jewellery was made in the Roman town of 'Eburacum' (York). It was very popular in parts of what is now Germany. Traders from York must have taken it there. Some **enamelled brooches** were also sold there. Other British **merchants** took lead, cloth, skins and oysters abroad to sell.

Glossary

altar a stone on which sacrifices were made to Roman gods

Anglo-Saxons people who settled in Britain at the end of the Roman Empire

archaeologists people who dig up and study things made in the past

brooch jewellery used to fasten clothing together. This was important in the days before zips and buttons.

craftworkers skilled people who are able to make useful or expensive objects

Empire the large area of land ruled by the Romans. It covered a large part of Europe, North Africa and the Middle East. The ruler was called the Emperor.

enamel a brightly coloured, shiny surface, put on metal

estate a large area of farmland, owned by a rich person

fired when pottery is heated to make it hard

fortified made strong, and hard to attack. Cities had walls to fortify them.

Governor the person in charge of running Roman Britain. He was given the job by the Emperor.

hillforts defended hilltops. Places where many British rulers lived before the Roman invasion of Britain.

industry work to make and sell things

jet a hard, black stone used to make jewellery. It could be carved and polished.

Legion a large group of Roman soldiers trained to work and fight together

magistrates people with the job of running Roman towns

merchant a person who travels to buy and sell things

mosaics floor pictures made from small pieces of stone

ore rock containing metal

pottery bowls, plates and bottles made from clay which is heated in an oven to make it hard

sacrifice giving something to God, or the gods. This would sometimes mean killing an animal or burning something.

settlement a group of houses, where people live together

shale a type of rock. It can be carved and polished.

slave someone who belongs to another person and has no freedom

taxes money paid to the government

trade buying and selling things

villa a large Roman house in the countryside

Timeline – Romans, Anglo-Saxons and Vikings

Roman Age

100BC	**AD1**
AD1	**AD43** Romans invade Britain
AD100	**AD49** First Roman town set up at 'Camulodunum' (Colchester)
AD200	**AD100**
AD300	**AD122** Romans start building Hadrian's Wall
AD400	**AD200**
AD500	More towns begin to have walls built round them
AD600	**AD300** Many rich villas built in the countryside
AD700	Most Roman pottery made in four main areas, by this time
AD800	**AD400**
AD900	**AD410** Britain stops being part of the Roman Empire
AD1000	**AD450** Parts of eastern Britain taken over by Anglo-Saxons

Index

Numbers in plain type (27) refer to the text. Numbers in italic type (16) refer to a caption.